My Notes

My Notes

My Notes

My Notes

My Notes

My Notes

My Notes

My Notes

My Notes

My Notes

My Notes

My Notes

My Notes

My Notes

My Notes

My Notes

My Notes

My Notes

My Notes

My Notes

My Notes

My Notes

My Notes

My Notes

My Notes

My Notes

My Notes

My Notes

My Notes

My Notes

My Notes

My Notes

My Notes

My Notes

My Notes

My Notes

My Notes

My Notes

My Notes

My Notes

My Notes

My Notes

My Notes

My Notes

My Notes

My Notes

My Notes

My Notes

My Notes

My Notes

My Notes

My Notes

My Notes

My Notes

My Notes

My Notes

My Notes

My Notes

My Notes

My Notes

My Notes

My Notes

My Notes

My Notes

My Notes

My Notes

My Notes

My Notes

My Notes

My Notes

My Notes

My Notes

My Notes

My Notes

My Notes

My Notes

My Notes

My Notes

My Notes

My Notes

My Notes

My Notes

My Notes

My Notes

My Notes

My Notes

My Notes

My Notes

My Notes

My Notes

My Notes

My Notes

My Notes

My Notes

My Notes

My Notes

My Notes

My Notes

My Notes

My Notes

www.ingramcontent.com/pod-product-compliance
Lightning Source LLC
LaVergne TN
LVHW021052100526
838202LV00083B/5834